Lace new style

Gerda Perik

FORTE PUBLISHERS

Contents

© 2002 Forte Uitgevers, Utrecht
© 2002 for the translation by the publisher
Original title: *Lacé nieuwe stijl*

ISBN 90 5877 217 9

This is a publication from
Forte Publishers BV
Boothstraat 1c
3512 BT Utrecht
The Netherlands

For more information about the creative books available from
Forte Uitgevers:
www.hobby-party.com

Publisher: Marianne Perlot
Editor: Hanny Vlaar
Photography and digital image editing: Fotografie Gerhard Witteveen, Apeldoorn, the Netherlands
Cover and inner design:
Studio Herman Bade BV, Baarn, the Netherlands

Preface

This is my fourth book about the Lacé cutting and folding technique. Once again, I have written this book with great enthusiasm. The twelve new templates which I have used in this book allow you to make many creative cards.

This time, I have only occasionally used ready-made duo-colour paper. For most of the cards, I have chosen two different colours of thin paper and stuck them together using spray adhesive. This gives you even more choice for combining pretty 3D pictures with attractively coloured paper.

I bet you can't wait to get started.

Gerda

Thanks:
Firstly, Marianne Perlot for her enthusiastic support. Our daughter Mariëlle for helping with the text, Mike for his good advice and Dini for helping with the cutting.

Techniques

Lacé cutting

The pattern to be cut out is shown on the light green Lacé templates, but you do not have to stick to the pattern. Some templates have nine different grooves, which can be used to produce nine different patterns. Always start counting from the template's smallest groove and write the numbers on the template using an indelible felt-tip pen (no. 1 is the smallest groove and no. 9 is the largest groove). Stick the template to the card using non-permanent adhesive tape or masking tape. Use a Lacé knife to cut along the grooves, starting at the point and cutting towards the outside. Always use a knife with a sharp point. After cutting, carefully remove the template from the card. It is important that you first score the edges which are going to be folded using the Lacé scoring and folding tool. Fold every other edge towards you and fold them under the edges that you have not scored. The patterns made from the narrow, straight Lacé templates cannot be folded under each other. These edges can only be folded and stuck down using a small amount of glue or double-sided adhesive tape.

Making your own duo-colour paper

Duo-colour paper is the prettiest paper to use for Lacé cutting, because each side has a different colour. This paper can be purchased in attractive colours, but you can also make it yourself. To do so, use paper which is no heavier than 120 gram per m2. Thinner paper can also be used. Lay a sheet of paper in a box and spray it with spray adhesive. It is important that you allow the paper to dry properly. Do the same to the other piece of paper. Stick the two sheets together and carefully rub them together.

Text vellum/printed parchment paper

You will always see traces of glue when using glue or double-sided adhesive tape with this type of transparent paper. Therefore, spray the vellum with spray adhesive (see above) and stick it on the card once the glue is almost dry.

Eyelets and flower-shaped eyelets

These are available in thirty different colours and have many different uses, such as decorating cards and attaching card decorations. They also look nice when a ribbon has been threaded through them. Instructions: make a hole with tool 1 using a hammer and a small plank of wood. Push the eyelet into the hole. Turn the card over and hit the ring open at the back using the hammer and

1. Stick two sheets of paper together using spray adhesive.

2. The new templates and Lacé cutting sheets.

3. Different possibilities using one template.

4. Decorate the card with pictures from cutting sheets.

tool 2. Gently hit the flower-shaped eyelet on the front again to make it slightly flatter.

Border stickers and sticky dots
The edges of many of the cards are decorated with border stickers. After removing gold and silver stickers from the background sheet, small dots are often left behind. Remove these dots with the end of your knife and stick them on the card.

3D cutting sheets
Cutting instructions are given for most of the pictures, but carry out the following if you use other pictures. Cut out all of the first picture and stick it on the card. For the second layer, do not cut out the bits that are in the background. For the third layer, only cut out what is in the foreground. Slightly puff up the pictures using a shaping pen or your fingers. Stick them on the card by placing small drops of 3D glue on the back. Carefully place them on top of each other and gently push them down. Do not press too hard, otherwise you will loose the necessary distance between the pictures. Only one picture is used for some cards. If so, puff up the picture, place a drop of glue on the back and stick it on the card.

Materials

- Artoz paper: various colours (80 grams), abbreviated to A (Kars)
- Papicolor paper: mother-of-pearl paper, duo-colour paper and metallic paper, abbreviated to P
- Lacé templates no. 22 to 34.
- Pink (024) and blue (044) design paper with white dots (Hobby Totaal)
- Pink aromatic paper,

- Gold card
- Text vellum/printed parchment paper
- Lacé knife
- Lacé scoring and folding tool
- Marianne Design and Marjoleine cutting sheets
- Eyelets and flower-shaped eyelets, plus tool set (Vaessen)
- 3D glue/silicon glue and glue nozzle

- Masking tape
- Circle cutter
- Cutting mat, knife and ruler
- Ribbons
- Spray adhesive, photo glue and double-sided adhesive tape
- Punches: Rounder a and c
- Plastic ladybirds

Specific materials are stated for each card

Card on page 1

Artoz paper: mango (A575) and honey yellow (A243) (stick these together), lobster red (A545) • Flowers cutting sheet (SIL3D2201) • Lacé template no. 25
Make a double card (10.5 x 14.8 cm). Cut a strip of paper (11 x 21 cm). Fold the strip into a harmonica (see photograph) and cut a circle (Ø 9.2 cm) out of the middle section. Cut grooves 4, 3, 2 and 1 of the Lacé template in this circle. Cut out the pattern leaving a 2 mm border to make a flower. Stick this on a lobster red circle (Ø 9.5 cm) and then stick this inside the card. Stick the harmonica card on the card. Stick all of the tulip border on the card and then stick only the tulips on it using 3D glue.

Card on page 3

Papicolor mother-of-pearl paper: green (P143) and light green (P139) (stick these together) • Hollyhock Shake-It cutting sheet (IT 353) • Dark pink flower-shaped eyelets • Lacé template no. 28
Make a double card (10.5 x 14.8 cm). Cut a strip of paper (11 x 21 cm). Fold the strip into a harmonica (see photograph) and cut a circle (Ø 9.2 cm) out of the middle section. Cut grooves 6 and 4 of the Lacé template in this circle. Score and fold the edges and stick the flower-shaped eyelets in the pattern. Stick the circle in the card. Stick the harmonica card on the card. Stick 3D hollyhocks on the edges.

Blue and green cards

Thin dark blue paper (A417) and algae green paper (A367) are stuck against each other for all the cards (see Techniques). Gold card and gold stickers are used to give an extra effect.

1. Green card with a blue circle

Lacé template no. 25
Make a double card (14 x 14 cm). Cut a circle out of dark blue paper (Ø 10.5 cm), a circle out of gold card (Ø 10.2 cm) and a circle dark blue/green paper (Ø 9.9 cm). Cut grooves 4, 2 and 1 of the Lacé template in the smallest circle. Stick all the circles on top of each other.

2. Blue card with hearts

Lacé template no. 23
Make a double card (14 x 14 cm). Cut grooves 7, 5, 3 and 1 of the Lacé template in the middle of the card. Stick gold card (14 x 14 cm) inside the card.

3. Green card with an octagon

Lacé template no. 28
Make a double card (14.5 x 14.5 cm). Cut grooves 9, 8, 6, 5, 3 and 1 of the Lacé template in the middle of the card. Stick gold card (14.3 x 14.3 cm) inside the card. Cut a piece of blue paper (12 x 12 cm). Draw pencil lines 3.5 cm from each corner and cut off the corners to make an octagon. Use this to make a 0.5 cm wide frame and stick it around the Lacé pattern. Stick a sticker on the card, for example, the number 50. Stick a border sticker in the middle of the frame.

4. Blue card with a green circle

Lacé template no. 24
Make a double card (14 x 14 cm). Cut a circle out of gold card (Ø 10.2 cm) and a circle out of green/blue paper (Ø 10 cm). Cut grooves 6, 5, 3 and 2 of the Lacé template in the green/blue circle. Stick the two circles on the card and finish the card with a border sticker.

5. Elongated card

Lacé template no. 29
Make a double card (10 x 19 cm). Cut a strip from gold card (6.8 x 19 cm) and a strip from dark blue/green paper (6.5 x 19 cm). Cut grooves 7, 6, 4 and 1 of the Lacé template in the blue/green strip. Stick the strips on the card and add a text sticker.

Gift label

Lacé template no. 33
Make this card from scrap pieces of paper, a ribbon and a text sticker.

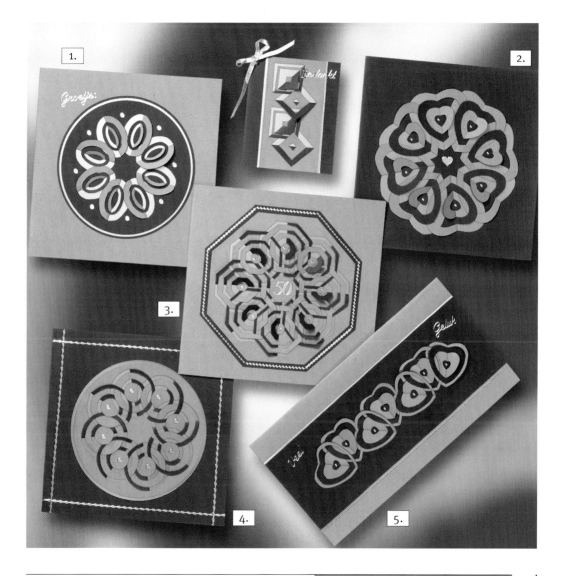

Purple cards

Purple/lilac Papicolor duo-colour paper (P182) is used for all the cards.

1. Pink roses
Pink aromatic paper • Lacé roses cutting sheet (Marianne Design) • Lacé template no. 24
Make a double card (13 x 13 cm). Cut a circle out of pink paper (Ø 11 cm) and a circle out of purple paper (Ø10.5 cm). Cut grooves 4 and 2 of the Lacé template in the purple circle. Stick the circles on the card. Use 3D glue to stick the roses on the card.

2. Purple flowers
Gold card • Lacé flowers cutting sheet (Marianne Design) • Lacé template no. 27
Make a double card (14 x 14 cm). Cut a circle (Ø 12 cm) out of the duo-colour paper. Cut all the grooves of the Lacé template in the lilac side of the circle. Stick gold circles (Ø 2 cm) in the corners of the pattern and stick flowers on the card using 3D glue.

3. Octagons
Flowers cutting sheet (SIL3D2201) • "Congratulations" text vellum • Lacé template no. 26
Make a double card (14 x 14 cm). Cut a piece of purple paper (10.5 x 10.5 cm). Draw pencil lines

3 cm from the corners and cut off the corners to make an octagon. Cut grooves 6, 5, 4 and 3 of the Lacé template in the octagon. Score and fold the edges and stick the octagon on lilac paper. Cut the octagon out leaving a 0.5 cm wide border. Stick everything on purple paper and cut it so that it is 0.5 cm larger than the lilac border. Stick this on the card and decorate the corners of the card with butterflies. In some

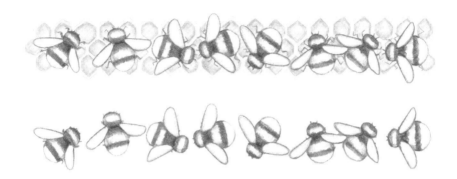

places, stick a second butterfly on the card using 3D glue. Stick a circle of text vellum (Ø 3.3 cm) in the middle.

4. Long card with bees

Gold/mother-of pearl paper (P141) • Yellow eyelets • Flowers cutting sheet (SIL3D2201) • Lacé template no. 30

Make a double card (11.5 x 19 cm). Cut a strip of gold/mother-of-pearl paper (6 x 19 cm) and a strip of duo-colour paper (5.5 x 19 cm). Cut the top grooves 6 and 4 of the Lacé template and the bottom grooves 6, 5, 4 and 2 in the second strip. Do this in turn (see example). Score and fold the edges and stick everything on the card. Finish the card with a 3D border of bees.

5. Purple tulips

Gold/mother-of pearl paper (P141) • Purple eyelets • Flowers cutting sheet (SIL3D2201) • Lacé template no. 32

Make a double card (12 x 17 cm). Cut a strip of gold/mother-of-pearl paper (15.2 x 17 cm) and a strip of lilac duo-colour paper (4.8 x 17 cm). The Lacé pattern is cut in the second strip: grooves 6 and 2 for the first pattern and grooves 6, 3 and 2 for the second pattern. Do this in turn. Stick the eyelets in the squares of the first pattern. Decorate the card with 3D tulip borders.

Gift label

Lacé template no. 34

Make small cards from scrap pieces of paper. Use the template to cut a couple of patterns. Score and fold them. Stick a flower-shaped eyelet in the middle of the pattern and tie a ribbon to the label.

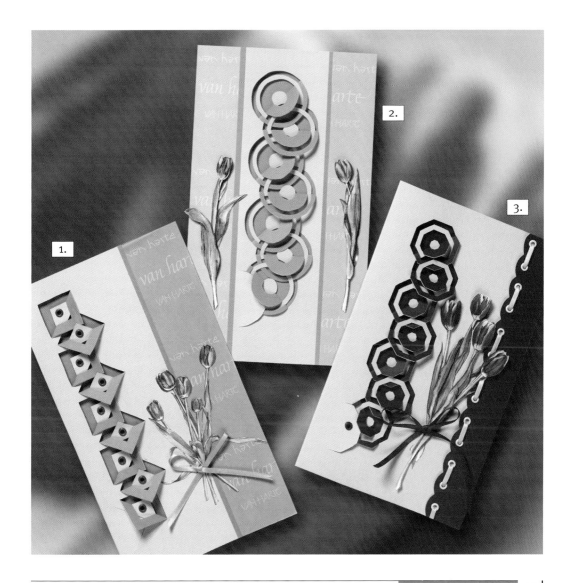

Tulip cards

Thin honey yellow paper (A243) is stuck against paper of a different colour (see Techniques) for these cards. All the cards measure 11.5 x 19.5 cm. The cards are finished with orange and purple tulips from Shake-It cutting sheets (IT 327 for the orange and purple cards and IT 328 for the red card).

1. Yellow and lilac card

Paper: lilac (A453) • White "Congratulations" text vellum • Lilac eyelets • Lilac ribbon • Lacé template no. 33

Cut grooves 6 and 4 of the Lacé template in the left-hand side of the double card. Stick an eyelet in the middle of each square. Cut a strip of lilac paper (4 x 19.5 cm) and a strip of text vellum (3.7 x 19.5 cm). Stick these strips against each other using spray adhesive (see Techniques) and then stick them on the card. Finish the card with a 3D bouquet of tulips and a ribbon.

2. Yellow and orange card

Paper: mango (A575) • White "Congratulations" text vellum • Lacé template no. 30

Cut grooves 6, 5, 4 and 1 of the Lacé template in the middle of the double card. Cut two strips of mango paper (3.2 x 19.5 cm) and two strips of text vellum (2.8 x 19.5 cm). Stick these strips against each other using spray adhesive (see Techniques) and then stick them on the left and right-hand sides of the card. Stick the tulips on the card and make them 3D.

3. Yellow and red card

Paper: red (A517) • Red and ecru eyelets • Yellow ribbon • Figure scissors • Lacé template no. 34

Cut grooves 7, 5, 3 and 1 of the Lacé template in the left-hand side of the double card. Stick an eyelet in the bottom groove. Cut a strip of red paper (3 x 19 cm) and cut a decorative border along it using the figure scissors. Stick an eyelet in the strip every 1.5 cm and thread a yellow ribbon through them. Stick the strip on the right-hand side of the card using thin foam tape. Finish the card with a 3D bouquet of tulips and a ribbon.

Ton-sur-ton

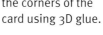

Thin honey yellow paper (A243) and mango paper (A575) are stuck against each other for all the cards (see Techniques).

1. Sunflowers

Paper: lobster red (A545) and bronze/metallic (P144) • Flowers cutting sheet (SIL3D2201) • Lacé template no. 32

Make a double card (10.5 x 14.8 cm). Cut a strip of bronze/metallic paper (5.5 x 14.8 cm), a strip of lobster red paper (5 x 14.8 cm) and a strip of honey yellow paper (4.5 x 14.8 cm). Cut grooves 6, 5 and 4 for the first Lacé pattern and grooves 6 and 5 for the second pattern in the honey yellow strip. Do this in turn. Stick the strips on the card. Stick the sunflower border on the card and make it 3D.

2. Circle with hearts

Paper: bronze/metallic (P144) • Butterfly cutting sheet (Marjoleine) • Lacé template no. 23

Make a double card (14 x 14 cm). Cut out two circles (Ø 12.5 cm): one from bronze/metallic paper and one from orange/honey yellow paper. Cut grooves 7, 6, 5 and 3 of the Lacé template in the orange/honey circle. Cut the pattern to the correct shape (see photograph). Stick the circles on the card. Stick butterflies in the corners of the card using 3D glue.

3. Butterflies

Paper: lobster red (A545) • Lacé butterflies cutting sheet (Marianne Design 6669) • Lacé template no. 28

Make a double card (14 x 14 cm). Cut a circle out of lobster red paper (Ø 12.3 cm) and a circle out of yellow/mango paper (Ø 11.8 cm). Cut grooves 9, 8 and 6 of the Lacé template in the yellow/mango circle. Stick the circles on the card. Decorate the card by sticking small butterflies to it using 3D glue.

4. Octagon

Paper: bronze/metallic (P144) • Lacé butterflies cutting sheet (Marianne Design 6669) • Lacé template no. 27

Make a double card (14 x 14 cm). Cut a piece of bronze/metallic paper (13 x 13 cm) and a piece of yellow/mango paper (12 x 12 cm). Cut grooves 6 and 4 of the Lacé template in the yellow/mango paper. Cut the pattern into a star shape 0.5 cm from the first groove. Stick the star on bronze/metallic paper and cut this out leaving a 0.5 cm border. Stick the layers on the card and stick a bronze circle (Ø 1.5 cm) in the middle. Stick some butterflies on the card using 3D glue.

1.

2.

3.

4.

5.

Green cards

Green/metallic paper (P143) is stuck against paper of a different colour for these cards (see Techniques).

1. Hearts and pumpkins

Paper: mango (A575) • Orange eyelets • Pumpkins cutting sheets (Marjoleine) • Lacé template no. 29
Make a double card (10.5 x 14.8 cm). Cut the Lacé template in the top and bottom of the card using only the three bottom hearts. Cut grooves 6, 4, 2 and 1 for the first pattern and grooves 6, 5, 2 and 1 for the second pattern. Do this in turn. Cut a strip of mango paper (4.5 x 10 cm) and a strip of green/metallic paper (4.2 x 9.7 cm). Stick the strips on top of each other on the card using the eyelets and stick the rectangle with the pumpkins on top of this. Make the picture 3D.

2. Octagon border

Paper: light green/mother-of-pearl (P139) • Dark pink eyelets • Rounder c punch • Sticky dots • Flowers cutting sheet (Marjoleine) • Lacé template no. 34
Cut part of the Lacé template in the left-hand side of the double card (10.5 x 14.8 cm). Cut grooves 7, 6 and 5 for the first pattern and grooves 7, 5 and 3 for the second pattern. Do this in turn. Stick the eyelets in the small octagons (see photograph). Cut two pieces of light green mother-of-pearl paper (3.5 x 3.5 cm). Punch out the corners and stick the 3D picture and the sticky dots on it.

3. Border of circles

Paper: yellow/mother-of-pearl (P141) • Pumpkins cutting sheet (Marjoleine) • Green and yellow eyelets • Lacé template no. 30
Make a double card (14.3 x 18 cm) and cut a window out of it (5.5 x 13 cm) 2.5 cm from the top and side edges and 3 cm from the bottom edge. Cut part of the Lacé template in the strip which you have cut out. Cut grooves 6, 4 and 1 for the first pattern and grooves 4 and 3 for the second pattern. Do this in turn. Stick eyelets in the circles. Stick the strip inside the card. Stick a 3 mm wide frame (5 x 12.5 cm) around the opening. Stick the square pictures with the 3D pumpkins on yellow/mother-of-pearl squares (5 x 5 cm) and stick eyelets in the corners.

4. Square card with flowers

Paper: light green/mother-of-pearl (P139) • Dark pink eyelets • Flowers cutting sheet (Marjoleine) • Sticky dots • Rounder c punch • Lacé template no. 27

Cut grooves 6, 5, 4 and 1 of the Lacé template in the middle of the double card (14 x 14 cm). Stick the eyelets in the corners of the pattern. Punch out the corners of a 0.5 cm wide light green/mother-of-pearl frame (13 x 13 cm). Stick the 3D picture in the corners and a red butterfly in the middle.

5. Pumpkins

Paper: mango (A575) • Pumpkins cutting sheet (Marjoleine) • Orange and green eyelets • Lacé template no. 24

Cut the Lacé template in the middle of the double card (14 x 14 cm). Cut grooves 6, 4 and 2 for the first pattern and grooves 4 and 3 for the second pattern. Do this in turn. Stick the eyelets in the circles (see photograph). Make a 3 mm

wide frame (10.5 x 10.5 cm). Stick 3 mm wide strips along the edges of the card. Make the pictures 3D.

Gift label

Lacé template no. 34

Make this card using scrap pieces of paper, flower-shaped eyelets and a ribbon.

Baby cards

Two sheets of thin paper are stuck together for these cards (see Techniques).

1. Baby bottles

Paper: royal blue (A427) and pastel blue (A413) • Party cutting sheet (SIL3D2203) • White "Congratulations" text vellum • Lacé template no. 34

Cut part of the Lacé template in the middle of the double card (14 x 15 cm). Cut grooves 7, 6, 5, 3 and 1 for the first pattern and grooves 7, 5, 3 and 1 for the second pattern. Cut a window (4.2 x 12 cm) in the text vellum (13.5 x 14.5 cm) and stick it on the card (see Techniques). Stick borders of bottles on the card and make the bottles 3D.

2. Safety pins

Paper: pink (A481) and cerise (100 gram) (P33) • White "Congratulations" text vellum • Party cutting sheet (SIL3D2203) • Lacé template no. 30

Cut the Lacé template in the middle of the double card (12.5 x 18 cm). Cut grooves 6, 5, 4, 3, 2 and 1 for the first pattern and grooves 4, 3 and 1 for the second pattern. Cut a window (5.2 x 13 cm) in the text vellum (12.5 x 18.5 cm) and stick it on the card (see Techniques). Decorate the card with safety pins.

3. For a daughter

Paper: wine red (A519) and pink (A481) • Pink paper with white dots (Hobby Totaal 024) • Mini cutting sheet (3D AM 1003) • Lacé template no. 27

Make a double card (14 x 14 cm). Cut a circle out of pink paper with white dots (Ø 12 cm) and a circle out of pink/wine red paper (Ø 11 cm). Cut grooves 6, 5, 3 and 1 of the Lacé template in the pink/wine red circle. Stick both circles on the card and stick various baby pictures on them using 3D glue.

4. For a son

Paper: dark blue (A417) and pastel blue (A413) • Blue paper with white dots (Hobby Totaal 044) • Mini cutting sheet (3D AM 1003) • White eyelets • Lacé template no. 26

Make a double card (14 x 14 cm). Cut a piece of paper (12 x 12 cm). Draw pencil lines 3.5 cm from the corners and cut the corners off to make an octagon. Cut grooves 6, 5, 4 and 1 of the Lacé template in this octagon. Stick the eyelets in the pattern. Stick the octagon on blue paper with white dots and cut it out leaving a 0.5 cm wide border. Stick the baby pictures on the card using 3D glue.

1.

2.

3.

4.

Text vellum

Two sheets of thin paper are stuck together for these cards (see Techniques).

1. Christmas star

Paper: royal blue (A427) and white (A211) • Gold origami paper • White text vellum • Lacé Christmas cutting sheet (Marianne Design 6666) • Lacé template no. 27

Make a double card (14 x 14 cm). Stick text vellum (13 x 13 cm) on the card (see Techniques). Cut grooves 6 and 4 of the Lacé template in a scrap piece of royal blue/white paper and cut it out leaving a 0.5 cm border. Stick the star on origami paper and cut it out leaving a 2 mm border. Stick the layers on the card and stick a gold circle (Ø 2 cm) in the middle. Stick Christmas decorations on the card using 3D glue.

2. Icicles

Paper: green (P18) and light green/mother-of-pearl (P139) • White text vellum • Gold card • Shake-It cutting sheet (IT 360) • Gold eyelets • Border sticker • Lacé template no. 34

Cut a window (5 x 13 cm) in a double card (14.5 x 18 cm). Cut grooves 7, 6 and 5 of the Lacé template in the piece of card which has been cut out. Stick eyelets in the pattern and stick the strip on a piece of gold card of the same size. Stick this strip inside the card. Stick text vellum on the front of the card. Cut the window out and stick a decorative border around it. Tie the Christmas decorations to an eyelet using a ribbon.

3. Merry Christmas

Paper: red (A517) and gold • Red text vellum • Lacé template no. 27

Make a double card (14.5 x 20 cm) and stick text vellum on it. Cut grooves 6, 4 and 2 of the Lacé template in a red/gold square (14 x 14 cm). Cut the pattern out leaving a 0.5 cm border. Stick the star on gold card and cut it out leaving a 0.5 cm border.

4. Christmas tree

Paper: dark blue (A417) and gold • Blue text vellum • Star stickers and line stickers • Shake-It cutting sheet (IT 358) • Lacé template no. 30

Cut a piece of dark blue/gold card (14.5 x 18 cm). Cut a window (5 x 13 cm) 2.5 cm from the top, bottom and left-hand edges. Cut part of the Lacé template in the rectangle which has been cut out. Cut grooves 6, 5, 3 and 1 for the first pattern and grooves 6, 5, 3, 2 and 1 for the second pattern. Stick the strip inside the card.

Stick text vellum on the card (see Techniques) and cut out the window. Stick a decorative border on the card and add a Christmas tree using 3D glue.

5. Border of stars

Paper: ivory/gold duo-colour paper • Dark red text vellum • Candles Shake-It cutting sheet (IT 356) • Line and star stickers • Lacé template no. 22

Cut a circle (Ø 9 cm) out of a double card (14 x 14 cm). Cut the Lacé template in the circle which has been cut out. Stick the circle inside the card and stick a circle (Ø 2.7 cm) in the middle. Stick a flower candle on the card using 3D glue. Stick a border sticker around the edge of the window.

Christmas star cutting instructions

1.

2.

3.

4.

5.

Christmas cards

Thin sheets of coloured paper are stuck
against each other for cards 1, 3, 4 and 5
(see Techniques).

1. White poinsettia

Cloud paper: green (P18) and beige (P53) •
Christmas cutting sheet (SIL3D2204) • Gold star
stickers • Gold vellum • Lacé template no. 34
Cut part of the Lacé template in the middle of a
double card (10.5 x 14.8 cm) using grooves 7, 5,
3 and 1. Stick gold vellum (10.2 x 14.5 cm) inside
the card. Finish the card with a border of 3D
poinsettias and stick star stickers on them.

2. Red card with a bow

Paper: red (A517) and gold vellum • Christmas
cutting sheet (SIL3D2204) • Gold star stickers
• Gold eyelets • Green ribbon • Lacé template
no. 33
Cut a 15 cm high strip lengthways from an A4
sheet of card. Draw a pencil line in the middle
and fold the sides towards the middle. Cut a
strip (7.5 x 15 cm) from a scrap piece of
red/gold paper and cut part of the Lacé pattern
in this strip. Cut grooves 6, 4, 3 and 2 of the
Lacé pattern for the first pattern and grooves 6,
5, 4, 3 and 1 for the second pattern. Stick the
strip on the card. Stick a 3 mm wide strip on the
left and right-hand sides. Stick an eyelet in both
sides and thread a ribbon through them.

3. Red card with a circle

Paper: red (A517) and green (P18) • Gold origami
paper • Lacé Christmas cutting sheet (Marianne
Design 6666) • Lacé template no. 27
Make a double card (14 x 14 cm). Cut a circle
out of gold paper (Ø 12.5 cm) and a circle out
of red/green paper (Ø 11.8 cm). Cut grooves 6,
5, 4 and 3 of the Lacé template in the red/green
circle. Stick the circles on the card. Finish the
card with Christmas pictures which are stuck on
the card using 3D glue.

4. Merry Christmas

*Paper: red (A517) and green (P18) • Gold vellum
• Red text vellum • Star stickers • Cutting sheet
(SIL3D2204) • Lacé template no. 22*

Make a double card (14.8 x 14.8 cm). Cut a
window (9.5 x 9.5 cm) out of the middle.
Cut the Lacé template in the square which has
been cut out. Stick gold vellum (10 x 10 cm)
behind it and stick the square in the card.
Decorate the Lacé border with star stickers.
Make a 2 mm wide frame (14.2 x 14.2 cm) from
gold vellum and stick this and some of the text
vellum on the card. Decorate the edge of the
card with 3D holly.

5. Lights

*Cloud paper: green (P50) and green (P18) •
Cutting sheet (SIL3D2204) • Line stickers • Gold
eyelets • Gold vellum • Lacé template no. 30*

Make a double card (11.5 x 19 cm) and cut a
window (6 x 14.5 cm) out of the middle. Cut
grooves 6 and 3 of the Lacé template in the
strip which has been cut out. Stick eyelets in
the pattern and stick gold vellum behind the
strip. Stick the strip inside the card. Decorate
the edges of the card with Christmas branches
with candles. Cut out the candles again and
stick them on the card using 3D glue.

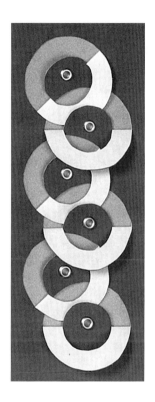

Gift label

Lacé template no. 33

Cut part of the Lacé template in a scrap piece of
paper. Tie a ribbon to the card.

Flower cards

Thin fawn paper (A241) and wine red paper (A519) are stuck against each other for all the cards. Stick the flowers (from Marianne Design cutting sheets) on the card using 3D glue and finish the cards with gold border stickers.

1. Flowers
Lacé flowers cutting sheet (6667) • Border stickers • Lacé template no. 28
Make a double card (14.5 x 14.5 cm). Cut a square piece of card (12.5 x 12 cm). Draw a pencil line 3.5 cm from the corners and cut the corners off to make an octagon. Cut grooves 9 and 7 of the Lacé template in this octagon. Stick a wine red circle (Ø 2 cm) in the middle. Stick squares which have been cut diagonally through the middle in the corners of the card: fawn (3 x 3 cm) and wine red (2 x 2 cm).

2. Tulips
Lacé tulips cutting sheet (6668) • Border stickers • Lacé template no. 25
Make a double card (14 x 14 cm). Cut a circle out of wine red paper (Ø 12.5 cm) and a circle out of fawn paper (Ø 10 cm). Cut grooves 5, 4, 3 en 1 of the Lacé template in the fawn circle. Cut the pattern out leaving a 1 cm wide border. Make the border curved instead of pointed. Stick the flower on the wine red circle and cut it out leaving a 1 cm border.

3. Hearts card
Gold paper • Lacé flowers cutting sheet (6667) • Lacé template no. 23
Make a double card (14.5 x 14.5 cm). Cut a circle out of gold paper (Ø 13 cm) and a circle out of fawn/wine red paper (Ø 13.8 cm). Cut grooves 7 and 5 of the Lacé template in the last circle.

4. Square Lacé pattern
Burgundy eyelets • Lacé tulips cutting sheet (6668) • Border stickers • Lacé template no. 32
Make a double card (10.5 x 14.8 cm). Cut grooves 6, 5, 4 and 1 of the Lacé template in a strip of paper (5 x 14.8 cm). Note: start with the second pattern. Cut out three fawn squares (4 x 4 cm) and stick eyelets in the corners.

5. Hydrangeas
Lacé flowers cutting sheet (6667) • Border stickers • Lacé template no. 27
Make a double card (14 x 14 cm). Cut a wine red/fawn square (12 x 12 cm) and cut grooves 6 and 4 of the Lacé template in this. Stick a fawn circle (Ø 2 cm) in the middle.

Gift label
Lacé template no. 34
Make this from scrap pieces of paper.

1.

2.

3.

4.

5.

Good luck

Thin sheets of coloured paper are stuck against each other for cards 2, 3, 4 and 5 (see Techniques). Pictures from the party cutting sheet (SIL3D2203) are used for the borders.

1. Hearts card

Lilac/purple duo-colour paper (P182) • Cutting sheet (3D 312) • Lacé template no. 29
Make a double card (13 x 13 cm). Cut the bottom three patterns of the Lacé template in the card. Cut grooves 6, 5, 4, 3 and 2 for the first pattern and grooves 6 and 5 for the second pattern. Finish the card with 3D pictures and stick the hearts on the card using 3D glue.

2. Wedding rings

Paper: wine red (A519), pink hearts, gold and scraps of pink paper • Lacé template no. 27
Cut a circle (Ø 10.8 cm) out of a double card (14.5 x 19 cm). Cut the Lacé border in the circle which has been cut out. Stick this (with the pink lines vertical) and a wine red circle (Ø 11.5 cm) inside the card. Stick a 0.5 cm wide round gold frame (outer diameter 10.8 cm) around the opening. Cut two pink strips (2.8 x 14.5 cm) and two gold strips (2.5 x 14.5 cm). Stick these and the strip of wedding rings on the card.

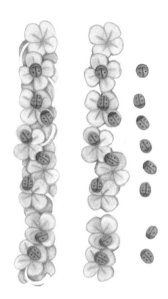

3. Champagne glasses

Paper: wine red/metallic (P146), pink (A481) and bright pink (P15) • Lacé template no. 27
Make a double card (14.5 x 14.5 cm). Cut the Lacé border in the middle of the card. Stick bright pink paper against the inside on the left-hand side of the card. Stick the border of glasses on a strip of wine red card and then on a strip of bright pink card and cut it out each time leaving a 1 mm border. Glue the two bright pink strips (2.8 x 12.5 cm) on the card and stick a couple of glasses on the card using 3D glue.

4. Ladybirds

Paper: bronze/metallic (P144) and gold/mother-of-pearl (P141) • Ladybirds • Lacé template no. 34

Cut the Lacé border in the middle of the double card (12 x 18.5 cm). Cut grooves 7, 6, 4 and 2 for the first pattern and grooves 7, 6, 5 and 3 for the second pattern. Do this in turn. Cut two strips of gold/mother-of-pearl paper (2.5 x 18.5 cm) and stick a strip with the clover on them. Stick some plastic ladybirds on the card using 3D glue.

5. Circle with hearts

Paper: bronze/metallic (P144) and gold/mother-of-pearl (P141) • Lacé template no. 23

Make a double card (14 x 14 cm). Cut a circle (Ø 13 cm). Cut grooves 7, 6, 4 and 2 of the Lacé template in this circle. Stick the circle on a gold/mother-of-pearl circle (Ø14 cm). Stick the cloverleaves on the card using 3D glue. Stick the ladybirds on the card again using 3D glue.

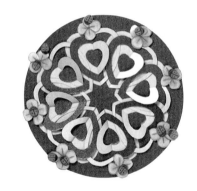

1.

2.

3.

4.

5.

Special thanks to Kars & Co B.V. in Ochten, the Netherlands, Vaessen Creative in Nuth, the Netherlands, Papicolor in Utrecht, the Netherlands, and Hobby Totaal in Zwolle, the Netherlands, for supplying the materials. Shopkeepers can order the material from: Kars & Co B.V. in Ochten, the Netherlands.